RANDOM AKROSTICS

RANDOM ACROSTIC POEMS BY KC

KC Rivera

BookLeaf Publishing

India | USA | UK

random aKrostiCs

random acrostic poems by KC

© 2021 KC Rivera

Presentation by BookLeaf Publishing

Web: www.bookleafpub.com

E-mail: info@bookleafpub.com

ISBN: 9789358739138
First edition 2021

This book is dedicated to Mom AND Guevs, who financed this possibility and made sure I wrote a poem everyday. I hope you enjoy the effort, and thank you for always cheering me on while also keeping me grounded <3

ACKNOWLEDGEMENTS

First, thank you to BookLeaf Publishing for providing this wonderful opportunity. It was fun and most definitely worth it.

A very special thank you to my Mom and Dad for always encouraging me to chase my dreams, and to do so realistically. Also thank you for financing this book, I hope you liked it.

Thank you to my siblings for….being my siblings I guess. And by that I mean giving me advice, making me feel all types of emotion, and forcing me to be mature enough to me a good role model and offer good advice and life lessons.

Thank you to Spotify for providing me with the right mood playlists to write these poems, and to all the artists who sang amazing narrative songs that helped me reflect on my own life.

Thank you also to my line Sisters, for our experiences together that gave me the opportunity to reflect and grow, particularly through this experience.

And lastly, thank you to God for blessing me with good and challenging experiences that inspired me to write a poem. Without Him, I would have nothing to write about.

PREFACE

This book is filled with, as the title suggests, random poems in acrostic style. Well, I guess not completely random, as they were inspired by how I was feeling on that day. Some days I was angry, some days I was hungry, and some days I was just running late. I tried to vary them in length, but that proved a challenge in itself because I could not break free of the notion that poems needed to rhyme to some extent. Maybe in the next one, we can see some growth. I also wrote most of these poems with the hope that they would impart a little life lesson, so hopefully you notice them. Anyway, I hope you enjoy these poems and possibly get inspired to write your own little book, because this endeavor definitely has inspired me to continue expanding on my writing abilities. It was quite fun.

1. AWARE (PAST)

After feeding the good wolf inside, it might seem
   like the bad one has died.

   Peace, happiness, patience have won, and it
      seems like the battle is done,

What happens next is a tad bit confusing, after years
   of burying bad feelings

   Anger, frustration, retaliation are rising, it
      appears they've only been hiding

Another battle is brewing, could it be the good
   wolf's undoing?

   So long as this next fact remains true, there's
      no stopping what good can do

Relax, take a breath, and unwind, there is no point
   to being unkind

   Though it might be a struggle to care, it
      helps to just stay aware

Even when it feels good to be bad, where's the good
   when that fad has passed?

2. HOME (LOVE)

Home is where the heart is, or so they say, but can
the heart be in multiple places in just one day?

> Let's say there's a group, more than friends
> in the end, the "home away from home"
> that your heart will defend

Or out on the coast, with friends from afar, while
driving back to the Midwest, with family in a car

> One heart can't be shared, you might think
> to yourself, maybe thinking literally
> won't be much of a help

Might I mention the heavens, up there in the sky,
where my heart has and will be, even after I die

> Very well, the heart can be shared, among
> places and people, everywhere that we
> cared

Even though not physical, or in any way literal,
maybe the saying was meant to be spiritual

> Each heart finds a home, or should I say
> homes, so maybe it's okay to let the heart
> roam

3. RUSH

Racing through life can bad, but also good, take
  speeding through the dark like anyone would

Understand there's a balance, racing the right times
  takes a little talent

Slow it down for love and for fun, but avoid the
  sadness and struggle and that's when you've won

Hope you can master the rush and coast through
  life, but remember we grow from living through
  strife

4. LATE

Life comes and it goes, keeping us all on our toes

And more often than not, we need more time to take
our shot

Time is a construct made up by our minds, so that's
why they say that time really flies

Especially when we're late, who else can relate?

5. YUM

You're sitting, you're chilling, then a savory food
commercial you're viewing.

Up until this sign you were fine, not feeling the need
to dine

McNuggets and fries later, enjoying that great
flavor, that "yum" makes you thank the creator.

6. ALONE

After spending time working together, suddenly
    something cuts the tether

Life suddenly changes, the world suddenly hazes

On top to rock bottom, not even wanting to call
    them

Nothing left to do now, time to take a solo bow

Even independent, it isn't the end yet.

7. MUSIC

Melodies that match the mood, even playlists for
    when you cook your food

Using music to communicate feelings, or in silence
    when you need some healing

Songs that say what we can't, or purely made to let
    us dance

It's hard to imagine life without it, there'd be so
    much in life I'd have to omit

Carols, choirs, concerts and more, without music life
    would be such a bore.

8. ANGER

All at once, the world goes red, but it all happens
    inside your own head

Nothing is calming or really relaxing, everything in
    the world seems a little too taxing

Good and kind words cease to exist, there's nothing
    to do and you're left feeling pissed

Eventually an end will arrive, leaving space for
    kindness and growth to just thrive

Relaxation and peace are near, but beware the anger
    that all of us fear.

9. LOST

Life cannot be beautiful without parts being
  challenging

On occasion we lose moments among all the things
  we are managing

Staying positive seems hard when you've lost the
  good cards

Try and take a step back until your heart can find
  what you lack.

10. SMILE

Sunshine breaks through the window, spilling all
over the pillow

Making breakfast seems a little easier, as opposed to
days that are sleepier

In everything that is done, there seems to be a lot
more fun

Life has fallen into place today, as everything goes
the right way

Even though others might lead to a frown, days like
this turn it upside down.

11. PLAY

Papers and tests and work steal our remaining
    childhood years

Leaving us to mourn the park, the games, the
    freedom in tears

And yet there's nothing keeping us from taking
    back the day

Yearn no longer and just go out and play.

12. HALF

How do we keep going with half the passion?

Ambition got us here, but now it's gone, in typical
  mood-swing fashion

Like, is there even a point if we don't move forward
  with a whole heart?

Feelings change and it's better to go with half than
  none, to play it smart

13. NO

Not much is worse than being a yes-man, taking on
too much to handle

One solution is to simply say no, and only take on
what you can tackle

14. PAY

Purchases are made every day, by you and me and
everyone in between

And one of the things we struggle with is who
covers who because rude we don't want to seem

Yet we forget that it's the memories that matter, so
maybe to sharing we should be more keen

15. DO

Don't miss out on your dreams by refusing to start
on them

Only when you start will you avoid being numb
from delaying them

16. SUN

Shining brightly in the morning, or setting softly in
the end

Under its rays a smile appears, and up a prayer I
send

Nothing feels better or cheers me up faster than a
sunny day without wind

17. EAT

Every day the search for sustenance continues, some
    with ease and some without

Although once gained the question becomes to save,
    share, spend or waste

Though one should enjoy and savor a meal with
    gratitude, always without a doubt

18. MOM

Many women change overnight, going from
  ordinary to extraordinary

One day they have to raise the next generation, a
  weight no other can carry

Man must not forget who gifts their existence, for a
  world that disrespects a mother can be quite
  scary

19. WATER

When you hear the rushing streams, there is both
    peace and destruction

A perfect symbol of the futility of life, where greater
    forces are at work

To rebel against its almighty flow causes more
    harm than we should care to know

Everchanging, everlasting, never-ending, forever
    passing

Revered and feared, for us to mirror until our end is
    near

20. END

Everything here on Earth is finite, with a date set to
end the journey

Nothing stops the inevitable, whether it be an
asteroid or "natural" causes

Don't rush it for the time will come, and time does
not respond to hurry